The Sovereign Journal

A System for Clarity, Control, and Leadership

A J Moore | Sovereign Frequency

This is not a journal of expression. This is a journal of clarity.

Clarity creates alignment. Alignment produces results.

Use consistently. No urgency.

A System for Clarity, Control, and Leadership

A J Moore | Sovereign Frequency

This journal is a structured reflection tool. If emotional distress intensifies, pause and seek appropriate support.

Pause. Inhale 4. Hold 2. Exhale 6. Repeat 3 times.

What is verifiably true in this moment?

____

What is interpretation?

____

What data am I missing?

____

____

____

____

____

____

____

Pause. Inhale 4. Hold 2. Exhale 6. Repeat 3 times.

What is verifiably true in this moment?

____

What is interpretation?

____

What data am I missing?

____

____

____

____

____

____

____

Pause. Inhale 4. Hold 2. Exhale 6. Repeat 3 times.

What is verifiably true in this moment?

____

What is interpretation?

____

What data am I missing?

____

____

____

____

____

____

Pause. Inhale 4. Hold 2. Exhale 6. Repeat 3 times.

What is verifiably true in this moment?

____

What is interpretation?

____

What data am I missing?

____

____

____

____

____

____

____

Pause. Inhale 4. Hold 2. Exhale 6. Repeat 3 times.

What is verifiably true in this moment?

____

What is interpretation?

____

What data am I missing?

____

____

____

____

____

____

____

Pause. Inhale 4. Hold 2. Exhale 6. Repeat 3 times.

What is verifiably true in this moment?

____

What is interpretation?

____

What data am I missing?

____

____

____

____

____

____

Pause. Inhale 4. Hold 2. Exhale 6. Repeat 3 times.

What is verifiably true in this moment?

____

What is interpretation?

____

What data am I missing?

____

____

____

____

____

____

Pause. Inhale 4. Hold 2. Exhale 6. Repeat 3 times.

What is verifiably true in this moment?

____

What is interpretation?

____

What data am I missing?

____

____

____

____

____

____

Pause. Inhale 4. Hold 2. Exhale 6. Repeat 3 times.

What is verifiably true in this moment?

____

What is interpretation?

____

What data am I missing?

____

____

____

____

____

____

____

Pause. Inhale 4. Hold 2. Exhale 6. Repeat 3 times.

What is verifiably true in this moment?

____

What is interpretation?

____

What data am I missing?

____

____

____

____

____

____

____

Pause. Inhale 4. Hold 2. Exhale 6. Repeat 3 times.

What is verifiably true in this moment?

____

What is interpretation?

____

What data am I missing?

____

____

____

____

____

____

Pause. Inhale 4. Hold 2. Exhale 6. Repeat 3 times.

What is verifiably true in this moment?

____

What is interpretation?

____

What data am I missing?

____

____

____

____

____

____

Stabilize. Inhale 4. Hold 2. Exhale 6. Repeat 3 times.

Emotion Present: _______________

Intensity (1–10): _______________

Trigger Source: Event / Thought / Memory

Notes:

____

Stabilize. Inhale 4. Hold 2. Exhale 6. Repeat 3 times.

Emotion Present: _______________

Intensity (1–10): _______________

Trigger Source: Event / Thought / Memory

Notes:

____

____

____

____

____

____

____

____

Stabilize. Inhale 4. Hold 2. Exhale 6. Repeat 3 times.

Emotion Present: _______________

Intensity (1–10): _______________

Trigger Source: Event / Thought / Memory

Notes:

____

____

____

____

____

____

____

____

Stabilize. Inhale 4. Hold 2. Exhale 6. Repeat 3 times.

Emotion Present: _______________

Intensity (1–10): _______________

Trigger Source: Event / Thought / Memory

Notes:

____

____

____

____

____

____

____

Stabilize. Inhale 4. Hold 2. Exhale 6. Repeat 3 times.

Emotion Present: _______________

Intensity (1–10): _______________

Trigger Source: Event / Thought / Memory

Notes:

____

____

____

____

____

____

____

Stabilize. Inhale 4. Hold 2. Exhale 6. Repeat 3 times.

Emotion Present: _______________

Intensity (1–10): _______________

Trigger Source: Event / Thought / Memory

Notes:

____

____

____

____

____

____

____

____

Stabilize. Inhale 4. Hold 2. Exhale 6. Repeat 3 times.

Emotion Present: _______________

Intensity (1–10): _______________

Trigger Source: Event / Thought / Memory

Notes:

____

____

____

____

____

____

____

Stabilize. Inhale 4. Hold 2. Exhale 6. Repeat 3 times.

Emotion Present: _______________

Intensity (1–10): _______________

Trigger Source: Event / Thought / Memory

Notes:

____

____

____

____

____

____

____

Stabilize. Inhale 4. Hold 2. Exhale 6. Repeat 3 times.

Emotion Present: _______________

Intensity (1–10): _______________

Trigger Source: Event / Thought / Memory

Notes:

____

____

____

____

____

____

____

Stabilize. Inhale 4. Hold 2. Exhale 6. Repeat 3 times.

Emotion Present: _______________

Intensity (1–10): _______________

Trigger Source: Event / Thought / Memory

Notes:

____

____

____

____

____

____

____

Stabilize. Inhale 4. Hold 2. Exhale 6. Repeat 3 times.

Emotion Present: _______________

Intensity (1–10): _______________

Trigger Source: Event / Thought / Memory

Notes:

____

____

____

____

____

____

____

Stabilize. Inhale 4. Hold 2. Exhale 6. Repeat 3 times.

Emotion Present: _______________

Intensity (1–10): _______________

Trigger Source: Event / Thought / Memory

Notes:

____

____

____

____

____

____

____

Stabilize. Inhale 4. Hold 2. Exhale 6. Repeat 3 times.

Emotion Present: _______________

Intensity (1–10): _______________

Trigger Source: Event / Thought / Memory

Notes:

____

____

____

____

____

____

____

Stabilize. Inhale 4. Hold 2. Exhale 6. Repeat 3 times.

Emotion Present: _______________

Intensity (1–10): _______________

Trigger Source: Event / Thought / Memory

Notes:

____

____

____

____

____

____

____

____

Stabilize. Inhale 4. Hold 2. Exhale 6. Repeat 3 times.

Emotion Present: ________________

Intensity (1–10): ________________

Trigger Source: Event / Thought / Memory

Notes:

____

____

____

____

____

____

____

Stabilize. Inhale 4. Hold 2. Exhale 6. Repeat 3 times.

Emotion Present: _______________

Intensity (1–10): _______________

Trigger Source: Event / Thought / Memory

Notes:

____

____

____

____

____

____

____

Stabilize. Inhale 4. Hold 2. Exhale 6. Repeat 3 times.

Emotion Present: _______________

Intensity (1–10): _______________

Trigger Source: Event / Thought / Memory

Notes:

____

____

____

____

____

____

____

Stabilize. Inhale 4. Hold 2. Exhale 6. Repeat 3 times.

Emotion Present: _______________

Intensity (1–10): _______________

Trigger Source: Event / Thought / Memory

Notes:

____

____

____

____

____

____

____

____

Stabilize. Inhale 4. Hold 2. Exhale 6. Repeat 3 times.

Emotion Present: _______________

Intensity (1–10): _______________

Trigger Source: Event / Thought / Memory

Notes:

____

____

____

____

____

____

____

____

Stabilize. Inhale 4. Hold 2. Exhale 6. Repeat 3 times.

Emotion Present: _________________

Intensity (1–10): _________________

Trigger Source: Event / Thought / Memory

Notes:

____

____

____

____

____

____

____

Regulate first. Inhale 4. Hold 2. Exhale 6. Repeat 3 times.

Where is my energy currently allocated?

____

What feels depleting?

____

What can be reduced or reallocated?

____

____

____

____

____

____

____

____

Regulate first. Inhale 4. Hold 2. Exhale 6. Repeat 3 times.

Where is my energy currently allocated?

____

What feels depleting?

____

What can be reduced or reallocated?

____

____

____

____

____

____

____

____

Regulate first. Inhale 4. Hold 2. Exhale 6. Repeat 3 times.

Where is my energy currently allocated?

____

What feels depleting?

____

What can be reduced or reallocated?

____

____

____

____

____

____

____

____

Regulate first. Inhale 4. Hold 2. Exhale 6. Repeat 3 times.

Where is my energy currently allocated?

____

What feels depleting?

____

What can be reduced or reallocated?

____

____

____

____

____

____

____

____

Regulate first. Inhale 4. Hold 2. Exhale 6. Repeat 3 times.

Where is my energy currently allocated?

____

What feels depleting?

____

What can be reduced or reallocated?

____

____

____

____

____

____

____

Regulate first. Inhale 4. Hold 2. Exhale 6. Repeat 3 times.

Where is my energy currently allocated?

____

What feels depleting?

____

What can be reduced or reallocated?

____

____

____

____

____

____

____

____

Regulate first. Inhale 4. Hold 2. Exhale 6. Repeat 3 times.

Where is my energy currently allocated?

____

What feels depleting?

____

What can be reduced or reallocated?

____

____

____

____

____

____

____

____

Regulate first. Inhale 4. Hold 2. Exhale 6. Repeat 3 times.

Where is my energy currently allocated?

____

What feels depleting?

____

What can be reduced or reallocated?

____

____

____

____

____

____

____

____

Regulate first. Inhale 4. Hold 2. Exhale 6. Repeat 3 times.

Where is my energy currently allocated?

____

What feels depleting?

____

What can be reduced or reallocated?

____

____

____

____

____

____

____

____

Regulate first. Inhale 4. Hold 2. Exhale 6. Repeat 3 times.

Where is my energy currently allocated?

____

What feels depleting?

____

What can be reduced or reallocated?

____

____

____

____

____

____

____

Regulate first. Inhale 4. Hold 2. Exhale 6. Repeat 3 times.

Where is my energy currently allocated?

____

What feels depleting?

____

What can be reduced or reallocated?

____

____

____

____

____

____

____

____

Regulate first. Inhale 4. Hold 2. Exhale 6. Repeat 3 times.

Where is my energy currently allocated?

____

What feels depleting?

____

What can be reduced or reallocated?

____

____

____

____

____

____

____

Regulate first. Inhale 4. Hold 2. Exhale 6. Repeat 3 times.

Where is my energy currently allocated?

____

What feels depleting?

____

What can be reduced or reallocated?

____

____

____

____

____

____

____

Regulate first. Inhale 4. Hold 2. Exhale 6. Repeat 3 times.

Where is my energy currently allocated?

____

What feels depleting?

____

What can be reduced or reallocated?

____

____

____

____

____

____

____

____

Regulate first. Inhale 4. Hold 2. Exhale 6. Repeat 3 times.

Where is my energy currently allocated?

____

What feels depleting?

____

What can be reduced or reallocated?

____

____

____

____

____

____

____

____

Regulate first. Inhale 4. Hold 2. Exhale 6. Repeat 3 times.

Where is my energy currently allocated?

____

What feels depleting?

____

What can be reduced or reallocated?

____

____

____

____

____

____

____

Regulate first. Inhale 4. Hold 2. Exhale 6. Repeat 3 times.

Where is my energy currently allocated?

____

What feels depleting?

____

What can be reduced or reallocated?

____

____

____

____

____

____

____

____

Regulate first. Inhale 4. Hold 2. Exhale 6. Repeat 3 times.

Where is my energy currently allocated?

What feels depleting?

What can be reduced or reallocated?

Regulate first. Inhale 4. Hold 2. Exhale 6. Repeat 3 times.

Where is my energy currently allocated?

____

What feels depleting?

____

What can be reduced or reallocated?

____

____

____

____

____

____

____

Regulate first. Inhale 4. Hold 2. Exhale 6. Repeat 3 times.

Where is my energy currently allocated?

What feels depleting?

What can be reduced or reallocated?

Clear noise. 4–2–6 breathing. Three rounds.

Income: _______________

Obligations: _______________

Available Margin: _______________

What decision improves stability?

____

____

____

____

____

____

____

____

Clear noise. 4–2–6 breathing. Three rounds.

Income: _______________

Obligations: _______________

Available Margin: _______________

What decision improves stability?

____

____

____

____

____

____

____

Clear noise. 4–2–6 breathing. Three rounds.

Income: _______________

Obligations: _______________

Available Margin: _______________

What decision improves stability?

____

____

____

____

____

____

____

Clear noise. 4–2–6 breathing. Three rounds.

Income: _______________

Obligations: _______________

Available Margin: _______________

What decision improves stability?

____

____

____

____

____

____

____

____

Clear noise. 4–2–6 breathing. Three rounds.

Income: _______________

Obligations: _______________

Available Margin: _______________

What decision improves stability?

____

____

____

____

____

____

____

Clear noise. 4–2–6 breathing. Three rounds.

Income: _______________

Obligations: _______________

Available Margin: _______________

What decision improves stability?

____

____

____

____

____

____

____

Clear noise. 4–2–6 breathing. Three rounds.

Income: ________________

Obligations: ________________

Available Margin: ________________

What decision improves stability?

____

____

____

____

____

____

____

Clear noise. 4–2–6 breathing. Three rounds.

Income: _______________

Obligations: _______________

Available Margin: _______________

What decision improves stability?

____

____

____

____

____

____

____

Clear noise. 4–2–6 breathing. Three rounds.

Income: _______________

Obligations: _______________

Available Margin: _______________

What decision improves stability?

____

____

____

____

____

____

____

Clear noise. 4–2–6 breathing. Three rounds.

Income: _______________

Obligations: _______________

Available Margin: _______________

What decision improves stability?

____

____

____

____

____

____

____

Clear noise. 4–2–6 breathing. Three rounds.

Income: _______________

Obligations: _______________

Available Margin: _______________

What decision improves stability?

____

____

____

____

____

____

____

____

Clear noise. 4–2–6 breathing. Three rounds.

Income: _______________

Obligations: _______________

Available Margin: _______________

What decision improves stability?

____

____

____

____

____

____

____

Clear noise. 4–2–6 breathing. Three rounds.

Income: ________________

Obligations: ________________

Available Margin: ________________

What decision improves stability?

____

____

____

____

____

____

____

Clear noise. 4–2–6 breathing. Three rounds.

Income: _______________

Obligations: _______________

Available Margin: _______________

What decision improves stability?

____

____

____

____

____

____

____

Clear noise. 4–2–6 breathing. Three rounds.

Income: _______________

Obligations: _______________

Available Margin: _______________

What decision improves stability?

____

____

____

____

____

____

____

Slow the system. 4–2–6 breathing.

Where am I tempted to intervene?

What would observation provide?

What outcome is possible without interference?

Slow the system. 4–2–6 breathing.

Where am I tempted to intervene?

____

What would observation provide?

____

What outcome is possible without interference?

____

____

____

____

____

____

____

Slow the system. 4–2–6 breathing.

Where am I tempted to intervene?

____

What would observation provide?

____

What outcome is possible without interference?

____

____

____

____

____

____

____

Slow the system. 4–2–6 breathing.

Where am I tempted to intervene?

____

What would observation provide?

____

What outcome is possible without interference?

____

____

____

____

____

____

____

____

Slow the system. 4–2–6 breathing.

Where am I tempted to intervene?

____

What would observation provide?

____

What outcome is possible without interference?

____

____

____

____

____

____

____

Slow the system. 4–2–6 breathing.

Where am I tempted to intervene?

____

What would observation provide?

____

What outcome is possible without interference?

____

____

____

____

____

____

____

____

Slow the system. 4–2–6 breathing.

Where am I tempted to intervene?

____

What would observation provide?

____

What outcome is possible without interference?

____

____

____

____

____

____

____

Slow the system. 4–2–6 breathing.

Where am I tempted to intervene?

____

What would observation provide?

____

What outcome is possible without interference?

____

____

____

____

____

____

____

Slow the system. 4–2–6 breathing.

Where am I tempted to intervene?

____

What would observation provide?

____

What outcome is possible without interference?

____

____

____

____

____

____

Slow the system. 4–2–6 breathing.

Where am I tempted to intervene?

____

What would observation provide?

____

What outcome is possible without interference?

____

____

____

____

____

____

____

____

Slow the system. 4–2–6 breathing.

Where am I tempted to intervene?

____

What would observation provide?

____

What outcome is possible without interference?

____

____

____

____

____

____

____

Slow the system. 4–2–6 breathing.

Where am I tempted to intervene?

____

What would observation provide?

____

What outcome is possible without interference?

____

____

____

____

____

____

____

Slow the system. 4–2–6 breathing.

Where am I tempted to intervene?

____

What would observation provide?

____

What outcome is possible without interference?

____

____

____

____

____

____

____

____

Slow the system. 4–2–6 breathing.

Where am I tempted to intervene?

____

What would observation provide?

____

What outcome is possible without interference?

____

____

____

____

____

____

____

Slow the system. 4–2–6 breathing.

Where am I tempted to intervene?

____

What would observation provide?

____

What outcome is possible without interference?

____

____

____

____

____

____

____

No urgency. Breathe 4–2–6. Three rounds.

Date: _______________

Current State (1–10): _______________

Primary Focus:

____

One Clear Decision:

____

Energy Preserved:

____

____

____

____

____

____

____

____

No urgency. Breathe 4–2–6. Three rounds.

Date: _________________

Current State (1–10): _________________

Primary Focus:

____

One Clear Decision:

____

Energy Preserved:

____

____

____

____

____

____

____

No urgency. Breathe 4–2–6. Three rounds.

Date: _______________

Current State (1–10): _______________

Primary Focus:

____

One Clear Decision:

____

Energy Preserved:

____

____

____

____

____

____

____

____

No urgency. Breathe 4–2–6. Three rounds.

Date: _______________

Current State (1–10): _______________

Primary Focus:

____

One Clear Decision:

____

Energy Preserved:

____

____

____

____

____

____

____

No urgency. Breathe 4–2–6. Three rounds.

Date: _______________

Current State (1–10): _______________

Primary Focus:

____

One Clear Decision:

____

Energy Preserved:

____

____

____

____

____

____

____

No urgency. Breathe 4–2–6. Three rounds.

Date: _______________

Current State (1–10): _______________

Primary Focus:

____

One Clear Decision:

____

Energy Preserved:

____

____

____

____

____

____

____

No urgency. Breathe 4–2–6. Three rounds.

Date: _______________

Current State (1–10): _______________

Primary Focus:

____

One Clear Decision:

____

Energy Preserved:

____

____

____

____

____

____

____

____

No urgency. Breathe 4–2–6. Three rounds.

Date: _________________

Current State (1–10): _________________

Primary Focus:

____

One Clear Decision:

____

Energy Preserved:

____

____

____

____

____

____

____

No urgency. Breathe 4–2–6. Three rounds.

Date: ________________

Current State (1–10): ________________

Primary Focus:

____

One Clear Decision:

____

Energy Preserved:

____

____

____

____

____

____

____

No urgency. Breathe 4–2–6. Three rounds.

Date: _______________

Current State (1–10): _______________

Primary Focus:

____

One Clear Decision:

____

Energy Preserved:

____

____

____

____

____

____

____

No urgency. Breathe 4–2–6. Three rounds.

Date: _______________

Current State (1–10): _______________

Primary Focus:

____

One Clear Decision:

____

Energy Preserved:

____

____

____

____

____

____

____

____

No urgency. Breathe 4–2–6. Three rounds.

Date: _______________

Current State (1–10): _______________

Primary Focus:

____

One Clear Decision:

____

Energy Preserved:

____

____

____

____

____

____

____

No urgency. Breathe 4–2–6. Three rounds.

Date: _______________

Current State (1–10): _______________

Primary Focus:

____

One Clear Decision:

____

Energy Preserved:

____

____

____

____

____

____

____

No urgency. Breathe 4–2–6. Three rounds.

Date: _______________

Current State (1–10): _______________

Primary Focus:

____

One Clear Decision:

____

Energy Preserved:

____

____

____

____

____

____

____

____

No urgency. Breathe 4–2–6. Three rounds.

Date: _______________

Current State (1–10): _______________

Primary Focus:

____

One Clear Decision:

____

Energy Preserved:

____

____

____

____

____

____

____

No urgency. Breathe 4–2–6. Three rounds.

Date: _______________

Current State (1–10): _______________

Primary Focus:

____

One Clear Decision:

____

Energy Preserved:

____

____

____

____

____

____

____

____

No urgency. Breathe 4–2–6. Three rounds.

Date: _______________

Current State (1–10): _______________

Primary Focus:

____

One Clear Decision:

____

Energy Preserved:

____

____

____

____

____

____

____

No urgency. Breathe 4–2–6. Three rounds.

Date: _______________

Current State (1–10): _______________

Primary Focus:

____

One Clear Decision:

____

Energy Preserved:

____

____

____

____

____

____

____

No urgency. Breathe 4–2–6. Three rounds.

Date: _______________

Current State (1–10): _______________

Primary Focus:

____

One Clear Decision:

____

Energy Preserved:

____

____

____

____

____

____

____

No urgency. Breathe 4–2–6. Three rounds.

Date: _______________

Current State (1–10): _______________

Primary Focus:

____

One Clear Decision:

____

Energy Preserved:

____

____

____

____

____

____

____

No urgency. Breathe 4–2–6. Three rounds.

Date: _______________

Current State (1–10): _______________

Primary Focus:

____

One Clear Decision:

____

Energy Preserved:

____

____

____

____

____

____

____

No urgency. Breathe 4–2–6. Three rounds.

Date: ______________

Current State (1–10): ______________

Primary Focus:

____

One Clear Decision:

____

Energy Preserved:

____

____

____

____

____

____

No urgency. Breathe 4–2–6. Three rounds.

Date: _______________

Current State (1–10): _______________

Primary Focus:

____

One Clear Decision:

____

Energy Preserved:

____

____

____

____

____

____

____

No urgency. Breathe 4–2–6. Three rounds.

Date: _______________

Current State (1–10): _______________

Primary Focus:

____

One Clear Decision:

____

Energy Preserved:

____

____

____

____

____

____

____

____

No urgency. Breathe 4–2–6. Three rounds.

Date: _______________

Current State (1–10): _______________

Primary Focus:

____

One Clear Decision:

____

Energy Preserved:

____

____

____

____

____

____

____

____

No urgency. Breathe 4–2–6. Three rounds.

Date: _______________

Current State (1–10): _______________

Primary Focus:

____

One Clear Decision:

____

Energy Preserved:

____

____

____

____

____

____

____

____

No urgency. Breathe 4–2–6. Three rounds.

Date: _______________

Current State (1–10): _______________

Primary Focus:

____

One Clear Decision:

____

Energy Preserved:

____

____

____

____

____

____

____

No urgency. Breathe 4–2–6. Three rounds.

Date: _______________

Current State (1–10): _______________

Primary Focus:

____

One Clear Decision:

____

Energy Preserved:

____

____

____

____

____

____

____

No urgency. Breathe 4–2–6. Three rounds.

Date: _______________

Current State (1–10): _______________

Primary Focus:

____

One Clear Decision:

____

Energy Preserved:

____

____

____

____

____

____

____

____

No urgency. Breathe 4–2–6. Three rounds.

Date: _______________

Current State (1–10): _______________

Primary Focus:

____

One Clear Decision:

____

Energy Preserved:

____

____

____

____

____

____

____

No urgency. Breathe 4–2–6. Three rounds.

Date: _______________

Current State (1–10): _______________

Primary Focus:

____

One Clear Decision:

____

Energy Preserved:

____

____

____

____

____

____

____

____

No urgency. Breathe 4–2–6. Three rounds.

Date: _________________

Current State (1–10): ________________

Primary Focus:

____

One Clear Decision:

____

Energy Preserved:

____

____

____

____

____

____

____

No urgency. Breathe 4–2–6. Three rounds.

Date: ________________

Current State (1–10): ________________

Primary Focus:

____

One Clear Decision:

____

Energy Preserved:

____

____

____

____

____

____

____

____

No urgency. Breathe 4–2–6. Three rounds.

Date: _______________

Current State (1–10): _______________

Primary Focus:

____

One Clear Decision:

____

Energy Preserved:

____

____

____

____

____

____

____

No urgency. Breathe 4–2–6. Three rounds.

Date: _______________

Current State (1–10): _______________

Primary Focus:

____

One Clear Decision:

____

Energy Preserved:

____

____

____

____

____

____

____

____

No urgency. Breathe 4–2–6. Three rounds.

Date: ________________

Current State (1–10): ________________

Primary Focus:

____

One Clear Decision:

____

Energy Preserved:

____

____

____

____

____

____

____

No urgency. Breathe 4–2–6. Three rounds.

Date: _______________

Current State (1–10): _______________

Primary Focus:

____

One Clear Decision:

____

Energy Preserved:

____

____

____

____

____

____

____

No urgency. Breathe 4–2–6. Three rounds.

Date: ________________

Current State (1–10): _______________

Primary Focus:

____

One Clear Decision:

____

Energy Preserved:

____

____

____

____

____

____

____

No urgency. Breathe 4–2–6. Three rounds.

Date: _________________

Current State (1–10): _________________

Primary Focus:

____

One Clear Decision:

____

Energy Preserved:

____

____

____

____

____

____

____

____

No urgency. Breathe 4–2–6. Three rounds.

Date: ________________

Current State (1–10): ________________

Primary Focus:

____

One Clear Decision:

____

Energy Preserved:

____

____

____

____

____

____

____

Clarity compounds. Consistency reveals patterns. Patterns create control. Continue.

A J Moore | Sovereign Frequency